T0199035

Verses from the Heart

A Collection of Spiritually Inspired Poems for Children

By Nadine Pileggi

Illustrated by Joanna Cistulli

About the Author

Nadine Pileggi, (B.A., B.Ed.) has enjoyed teaching young children for over 25 years while living in Canada, Brazil and the United States. Currently she resides in Florida with her husband Francisco. Together, they love to spend time with their three daughters, their husbands and grandchildren.

Upon retirement, Nadine has written "Verses from the Heart," a spiritually inspired children's book. As children develop their reading skills, they will have an opportunity to grow in their faith through the verses. This educational book can be utilized as a teaching tool for parents, grandparents and teachers. It is Nadine's desire that you are blessed and encouraged as you personally experience the messages conveyed within her book.

Special thank you to Pawel Krzystof & Vanessa Pileggi for their assistance with this book.

Dedicated to our Heavenly Father, God, and His son, the Lord Jesus Christ, and the Holy Spirit. My loving family, friends, and you, the reader. May you be blessed by God's word.

WestBow Press books may be ordered through booksellers or by contacting:

WestBow Press
A Division of Thomas Nelson & Zondervan
1663 Liberty Drive
Bloomington, IN 47403
www.westbowpress.com
1 (866) 928-1240

Interior Image Credit: Joanna Cistulli

All Scripture quotations are taken from the King James Version.

ISBN: 978-1-9736-9550-9 (sc)
ISBN: 978-1-9736-9551-6 (e)

Library of Congress Control Number: 2020911817

Print information available on the last page.

WestBow Press rev. date: 02/27/2021

WESTBOW
PRESS®
A DIVISION OF THOMAS NELSON
& ZONDERVAN

In the Beginning

In the beginning of our world, God made everything.
He made the heavens and the earth. God made the
land and the water. He made the creatures on the
earth. God made people like you and me.
Thank you God for your wonderful work.

God Our Father's World

"In the beginning God created the heaven and the earth."

– Genesis 1:1 KJV

Father

God is my Father. God is your Father. He is
Father to everything on the earth.
He is the Father to everything in the heavens. Thank
you God, for being our heavenly Father.

Our Miracle God

You can do anything.
You can do everything.
You can help anyone.
You can help everyone.

The Word

"I Am" is God's name.

He gave us a wonderful gift.

His gift is his word.

Look for his words in the Bible.

The Bible is the book with God's word. Thank you God, for the gift of your word.

I Am

God's name is "I Am."

God has many names.

I can call, "I Am," God.

Thank you God, for letting me call you by name.

4

God Made Me

God knew me before I was born.

God made me just the way I am.

I am his finished work.

He made everything about me.

God knows my eye color.

He knows my hair color.

God knows me by name.

He is happy with me.

God loves me always.

Thank you God, for making your perfect me.

I love you.

I'm Me

God made me with his plan.

I have my own special gifts from God,

God put them on my heart.

Dear God, please help me to use my gifts wisely.

Our Love

God loved his world.

God gave us his son.

God's son is Jesus

God loves us.

Jesus loves us.

We love you and thank you God and Jesus.

Jesus is God's Son

"And lo a voice from heaven, saying,
This is my beloved Son, in whom I am well pleased."
– Matthew 3:17 KJV

God's Son

God's son is Jesus.

He is very special.

Jesus is a messenger.

Jesus is a friend.

Jesus loves you.

Thank you God, for your son Jesus.

Our Savior

Jesus is our savior.

He is God's son.

Jesus is a gift from God to us.

He is our key.

Jesus is our way to heaven.

Jesus is The Way

Jesus is the way.

He is the light.

Jesus is the truth.

He is the life.

Jesus died to help you and me.

Then he became alive again.

Jesus came to save us.

He shows us the way to heaven.

The Bible tells us how.

Loving Kindness

What is loving kindness?

It is loving.

It is kindness.

God shows loving kindness.

Jesus shows loving kindness.

We can show loving kindness too.

I am a Special Child

God made me special for a reason.

He formed me to have special gifts.

God gave me weaknesses and strengths.

He gave me abilities for sports and school. Sometimes

when I think of others, I forget about

the special qualities that my heavenly Father has given me.

Please God, help me to remember who I am. I am your child.

I am Special

I am God's child. I belong to him.

"Before I formed thee in the belly I knew thee..."

– Jeremiah 1:5 KJV

I am a Special Grandchild

God made me special for a reason.

He gave me special gifts.

I am special to my parents, and they love me.

I am special to my grandparents, and they are special to me.

I love my grandparents, and they love me.

Thank you God, for my parents and grandparents.

They are special gifts to me.

I am a Special Friend

God made me special for a reason.

I know He loves me very much.

God made me to be a special friend.

I can love others just like God loves me. I love

God and Jesus with all my heart.

Thank you God, for giving me a loving heart.

I am a Special Gift

God made me special for a reason.

It is because he loves me.

God made me one of a kind.

Nobody else is exactly like me.

Because I am myself,

I can make a difference in God's world.

Thank you God for making me the way you wanted me to be.

I am a Special Student

God made me special for a reason.

He gave me special gifts to use and grow.

God gave me the interest to learn in school.

He gave me the choice to have good work habits.

Dear God, please help me to use my gifts the way you would like me to.

Jesus Makes Me Strong

Jesus makes me strong.

His words give me courage.

He is always with me.

I am never alone.

We are two: Jesus and I.

Jesus and I make two.

Two together are strong.

Jesus is Always Near

"The Lord is my strength and song, and he is become my salvation..."
– Exodus 15:2 KJV

Jesus

His arms are outstretched to me.

He hugs me tight.

Jesus is wonderful.

I love him.

He is God's only son.

I want to be near him, always.

He calls my name.

I call his name.

We are friends.

Jesus loves me.

Jesus loves you.

Jesus is my Lord and Savior.

Jesus is my friend.

He is always near.

Jesus loves me.

He helps me.

Jesus is happy with me.

He watches over me.

Jesus sends his angels to watch over me.

Jesus smiles and winks at me.

Never Alone

In his word, God says that he will never leave me alone.

God and Jesus will always be by my side.

They will watch over me when I go out or come in.

They will watch over me day and night.

I can always be with God and Jesus.

Be Still

God tells us to keep ourselves still.

Then we will know that he is God.

You can go to a quiet place in your room.

You can keep your body completely still.

You can close your eyes.

You can think about God and his word.

My Help

God and Jesus are my friends and help.

They help me in times of trouble.

God and Jesus are there to see me.

They are there to listen to me.

God and Jesus want me to call on them.

When I need help, I can pray to them.

"And this is his commandment, That we should believe on the name of his Son Jesus Christ, and love one another, as he gave us commandment."

– 1 John 3:23 KJV

The Life of Jesus

When baby Jesus was born, the angels came down from heaven.

They were singing and praising God, because they believed.

The angels visited the shepherds in the fields to tell them the great news!

The shepherds believed that Jesus Christ was born, and went to worship him.

When Jesus was a baby, the wise men believed.

They believed that Jesus was the son of God. The

wise men believed that Jesus was King.

They came from far away to worship baby Jesus.

The wise men brought special gifts because they believed in baby Jesus.

They believed that Jesus was the savior.

As Jesus grew up, many people believed in him, as he spoke the word of God

He wanted to teach a special group of followers.

Jesus called twelve people to come and learn with him.

When Jesus called, each person came and followed him.

These people were called the twelve disciples.

Because the disciples believed in God and Jesus, so can I.

As Jesus traveled, many people believed in him, as he spoke the word of God.

People in the cities and country believed in Jesus' words.

People that were old and young, sick and well, came to hear Jesus speak.

The people that believe in Jesus Christ are called "Christians".

Because Christians believe in God and Jesus, so can I.

Jesus and his disciples traveled together around the countryside.

He taught people how to live as Christians.

Jesus performed many miracles.

The blind could see, the deaf could hear, because they believed.

The sick were well, the dead could live, because they believed.

Because they believed in Jesus, so can I.

Believe

I Can Believe

Because they believed, so can I.

Because people that came before me believed in God, so can I.

Abraham, Isaac, and Jacob believed in God.

Joseph, Noah, and Moses believed in God.

Esther, Ruth, and Mary believed in God.

Because they believed, so can I.

God sent his son to Mary and Joseph.

Mary and Joseph believed in their son Jesus.

Mary's Aunt Elizabeth and Uncle Zechariah believed in God and Jesus.

Their son, the cousin of Jesus, John the Baptist, believed.

King Jesus

King Jesus is alive and well forever.

He is eternal, and is always there for us. Jesus is

still performing miracles each day.

He is just a call away, whether in the day or night.

Because I believe in Jesus, so can you!

My Cup

My cup is so full, it is overflowing.

God is following me to fill my cup.

He wants to fill my life with blessings.

God gives me so many blessings, that my cup overflows.

Dear God, please remind me to be thankful

for your many blessings each day.

Each Perfect Day

God sends the painted sunrise.

His birds sing with joy.

God's spirit moves in the wind.

His trees sway with praise.

God's golden sun warms our hearts.

God is beauty.

God is love.

God's day is wonderful.

He sends the perfect sunset.

God gives us peace and rest.

I Can Learn About Jesus and God

I can learn about Jesus.

I can learn about what Jesus did.

I can learn about what Jesus said.

I can learn about what Jesus said to me.

I can learn about where Jesus lived.

I can learn about who he met.

I can learn about his stories.

I can learn about his helpers.

I can learn about his love.

I can tell others about Jesus.

"If any of you lack wisdom, let him ask of God, that giveth to all men liberally, and upbraideth not: it shall be given him."

– James 1:5 KJV

God's World

This is God's world. God made everything in it.

The Bible is God's word to us.

We can't see him, but he can see us.

Sometimes we can feel he is very near.

God never sleeps! He keeps watching the world day and night.

God sends his messenger, the Holy Spirit to us.

Sometimes the Holy Spirit speaks to our hearts.

The Holy Spirit helps us to think about God and Jesus.

When Jesus left the earth to be with his heavenly Father,

God, He left the Holy Spirit to be with us.

Thank you for sending the Holy Spirit.

I Can Read About Jesus

I can read about Jesus.

I can read about his Mother Mary.

I can read about his Father Joseph.

I can read about his heavenly Father, God.

I can read about Jesus all by myself.

Jesus' Words

Jesus' words are in the Bible.

I can read his words every day.

Jesus' words make me smart.

His words help me every day.

His words help me to help myself.

His words help me to help others.

If people have problems, they can read the Bible.

They can get help for everything.

Remember

God wants us to remember him when we are young.

He wants us to study his word in the Bible.

God wants us to learn and remember by heart.

He wants us to memorize his word.

Then when we grow up, we will remember and follow what he has written.

My Country's Birthday

Dear Lord, thank you for my country.

Today we celebrate our Nation's birthday.

We have freedom and democracy.

Thank you for the beautiful land.

Thank you for your wonderful people.

I love my country so much.

My heart fills with pride.

Our country is blessed.

May the Lord bless you

and your country.

Thank you, God.

Jesus is Lord

Jesus says to stay near him.

Be with him every night and day!

Keep close by reading his words and praying!

He teaches us to pray his prayer.

I can learn to say the Lord's Prayer all by myself.

I can say the Lord's prayer with others.

The Lord's Prayer

"After this manner therefore pray ye:

Our Father which art in heaven, Hallowed be thy name.

Thy kingdom come. Thy will be done in earth, as it is in heaven.

Give us this day our daily bread.

And forgive us our debts, as we forgive our debtors.

And lead us not into temptation, but deliver us from evil:

For thine is the kingdom, and the power, and the glory, forever.

Amen."

– Matthew 6:9-13

The Psalms

The Psalms are part of the Bible that say prayers.

Psalm 23 is a favorite for many people.

You can learn Psalm 23 all by yourself.

You can take it with you in your mind anywhere.

Psalm 23 will help you and make you strong.

Jesus is our shepherd in everything.

Psalm 23 was written by Kind David to honor God.

Psalm 23: The Lord is My Shepherd KJV

"The Lord is my shepherd; I shall not want. He maketh me to lie down in green pastures: he leadeth me beside the still waters. He restoreth my soul: he leadeth me in the paths of righteousness for his name's sake.

Yea, though I walk through the valley of the shadow of death, I will fear no evil: for thou art with me; thy rod and thy staff they comfort me.

Thou preparest a table before me in the presence of mine enemies: thou anointest my head with oil; my cup runneth over. Surely goodness and mercy shall follow me all the days of my life: and I will dwell in the house of the Lord for ever."

Jesus is King

Jesus says to follow him.

Jesus says that he is the way to follow.

Jesus tells the truth.

His life is the example of how to live.

Jesus is King.

Jesus is the King of the world.

He sits beside the right hand of God in Heaven.

Follow his word, and one day he will give you a crown.

Jesus looks after your family.

Jesus watches over all your family.

King Jesus Will Return

"And now, little children, abide in him: that, when he shall appear, we may have confidence, and not be ashamed before him at his coming."

– 1 John 2:28 KJV

Watchful Eyes, Listening Ears

God's word tells us that his son, Jesus will be coming to earth.

The trumpets will announce him.

Jesus is coming on a cloud.

He will land in the city of Jerusalem.

Everybody will see Jesus arrive!

God asks us to have watchful eyes and listening ears.

We should be watching and waiting, like a soldier on guard.

Thank you God, for sending Jesus.

The Wonderful Cloud

Jesus is coming back to earth on a cloud.

Can you hear the trumpets sounding?

Everyone in the world will look up.

Everybody will see.

We will be excited and happy.

Jesus is coming on a cloud.

You Can Pray to God and Jesus

You are alone in a quiet spot.

Your palms are open in praise.

Your eyes are closed.

You can feel God's presence.

You can say:

Thank you for my blessings,

Lord Jesus and Heavenly Father, God.

Please continue to bless me with your wisdom.

Please strengthen my faith, and increase my joy in you.

Let me be a shining light for you.

Amen.

Prayer

"Ask, and it shall be given you; seek, and ye shall find;

knock, and it shall be opened unto you:

For every one that asketh receiveth; and he that seeketh

findeth; and to him that knocketh it shall be opened."

– Mathew 7: 7-8 KJV

Jesus Loves Us

Jesus loves us.

He keeps us safe.

He teaches us.

We are happy being with Jesus.

He is with us day and night,

year after

year, forever!

Little Children

God loves little children.

Jesus loves little children.

Jesus said to bring the little children to him.

You can pray and talk to Jesus.

Jesus is waiting to hear from you and me,

any time of the day or night. Always!

God's Gifts

God gave us a free gift tonight.

What a beautiful eclipse!

It was awesome!

All of God's gifts are free.

Look in nature.

Look all around you.

God's biggest gift to us is salvation.

It was bought by his son, Jesus.

That is why it is free for us.

Thank you Lord Jesus, for your gift of salvation!

God's Gifts

"Every good gift and every perfect gift is from above, and cometh down from the Father of lights, with whom is no variableness, neither shadow of turning."

– James 1:17 (KJV)

Salvation Prayer

Dear Jesus.

Please come into my heart

And be my Lord and Savior.

Thank You.

Amen

Aaronic Blessing

"The Lord bless thee, and keep thee:

The Lord make his face shine upon thee, and be gracious unto thee:

The Lord lift up his countenance upon thee, and give thee peace."

– Numbers 6:24-26 (KJV)

Printed in the United States
By Bookmasters